A Healthy Body

A Book About Fitness and Nutrition

By Mary Packard

Illustrated by Joy Friedman

*Prepared with the cooperation of Bernice Berk, Ph.D.,
of the Bank Street College of Education*

*Pleno Moise, M.D., Pediatric and Adolescent
Medicine, Consultant*

A GOLDEN BOOK · NEW YORK

Western Publishing Company, Inc., Racine, Wisconsin 53404

Text copyright © 1986 by Mary Packard. Illustrations copyright © 1986 by Joy Friedman. Special material copyright © 1986 by Western Publishing Company, Inc. All rights reserved. Printed in the U.S.A. No part of this book may be reproduced or copied in any form without written permission from the publisher. GOLDEN®, GOLDEN & DESIGN®, A GOLDEN BOOK®, and A GOLDEN LEARN ABOUT LIVING® BOOK are trademarks of Western Publishing Company, Inc. Library of Congress Catalog Card Number: 86-80128. ISBN 0-307-23287-5/ISBN 0-307-63287-3 (lib. bdg.) A B C D E F G H I J

Note to Parents

The media is full of conflicting messages on the subject of health and fitness. TV ads showing the glamour of exercise appear alongside commercials in which the virtues of tempting, fattening foods are praised by large popular restaurant chains. Magazines may show an irresistible chocolate cake on their covers together with a new diet that will take off pounds faster than any other. What is a person to think?

If grown-ups are bewildered, it's even harder for kids to sort out these messages. There are some simple and obvious ways to counter these conflicting messages and help your family establish good eating and exercise habits. A good first step is to become interested in health and fitness issues yourself. It's also important to set good examples by eating and planning nutritious meals. Planning family outings that incorporate enjoyable exercise in imaginative ways, such as games, is also recommended.

Of course, kids may rebel when they are told that the foods, activities, and things they like are no good for them. An outright ban on so-called "junk foods" may simply lead a child to eat them secretly. (Some experts suggest that occasional eating of junk foods cannot undo the benefits of a regular diet of nutritious foods, so a good approach is to teach your child about the virtues of moderation and a balanced diet.) Similarly, turning off the TV and telling a child to go outside and get some exercise is not likely to produce a love of physical activity.

A parent's participation in these areas is the key to helping a child develop an awareness of the benefits of a healthy diet and exercise. Discussing why certain foods are better than others, in terms of how the body works, is important. So are informative talks about the rewards of exercise and physical activity. Once kids understand these things, it may be easier to appeal to their developing sense of reason. It's a challenge, but helping your kids establish healthy eating and exercise habits will start them off toward a lifetime of fitness.

—The Editors

Olivia and her brother, Oliver, couldn't agree on how to spend their day.

"Want to ride bikes?" asked Oliver.

"Nah, I can't find my sunglasses," answered Olivia. "How about jumping rope in the shade?"

"No! No! No! That makes me get all out of breath," said Oliver. "And sometimes I even start to sweat. I get tired just thinking about it. Why don't we just stay inside and watch TV?"

"Okay," said Olivia, "but only if I get to pick the program."

Olivia went to the freezer to get some ice cream. When she got back, she found her brother sitting in her favorite chair.

"Hey, no fair!" wailed Olivia.

Oliver was about to reply when a strange thing happened.

"Olivia…Oliver…" called a mysterious voice.

"Who's that?" Olivia whispered.

"'WHAT is that?' is a better question," gasped Oliver.

"I'm your fairy bodmother," said the voice.

"Don't you mean fairy godmother?" asked Olivia.

"No, I'm your fairy bodmother. I've come to help you take care of your bodies."

"What's wrong with my body?" asked Olivia indignantly. Oliver snickered in the background.

"Nothing, dear. Your body is perfect. Don't you want to keep it that way?" The two of them turned and saw a little lady standing on the mantelpiece. "Maybe if you learn a little about the way it works, you'll want to treat it better. Tell me something. Would you rather grow up to be a streamlined sports car with lots of pickup, or a sputtering old jalopy that stalls at every light?"

"That's easy," said Oliver. "It would be much more fun to be a sports car. But I still don't get it," he added.

"Just think of your body as a very fine engine," began the fairy. "The food you eat is its fuel. But before your body can use the food as fuel, it has to be processed through the long food tube inside you.

"First, your teeth grind the food up into tiny pieces. After it mixes with saliva, you can swallow it. Then down it goes into your stomach. Special juices in your stomach mix with the bits of food to make a soupy paste. Then the whole mixture gets pushed down again into a long, winding tube called your intestines. This is where the tiny bits of food finally get absorbed into your blood. Every part of your body needs fuel to keep on doing its job. Your blood carries the fuel wherever it's needed."

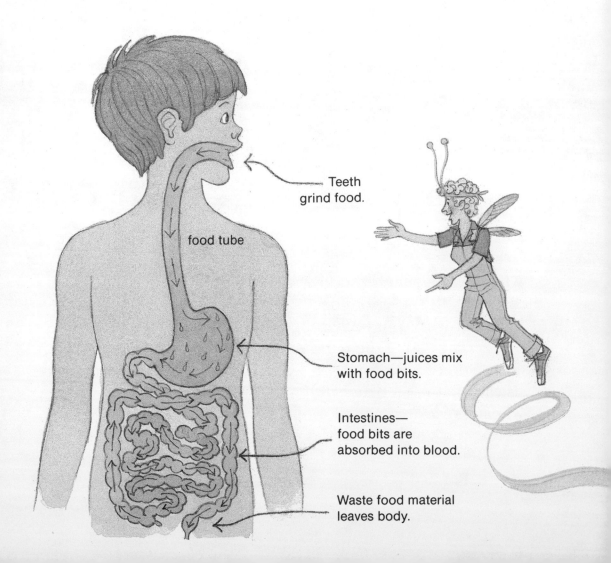

Teeth grind food.

food tube

Stomach—juices mix with food bits.

Intestines—food bits are absorbed into blood.

Waste food material leaves body.

"So, what kind of fuel would you put into a snazzy sports car—high-test or regular?" asked the fairy bodmother.

"High-test, of course," answered Oliver.

"Precisely," agreed the fairy. "That is, if you want to keep your body fit and running smoothly."

"You mean we have to drink high-test gasoline?" asked Olivia.

"Goodness, gracious me, no," sniffed the fairy. "What you have to do is eat what I call high-test foods—the kind that help you grow, stay healthy, and give you energy. Let's go shopping!"

She buzzed out the door. Olivia and Oliver had a hard time keeping up.

When they got to the supermarket, the fairy bodmother tore off down the aisle. "Did you know that your body is made of trillions of tiny building blocks called cells?" she said. "Cells come in different shapes and sizes, but one thing all these cells need to live is protein. So let's start by finding the bodybuilding foods that are made of protein, such as meat, fish, poultry, eggs, milk, cheese, nuts, and peas."

"Can't we buy some potato chips, too?" begged Olivia.

"That's low-test, Olivia. Fine for an occasional party, but they have very little of what your body really needs."

"How about some Caramel Crispies for breakfast?" wheedled Oliver.

"Real jalopy food," snapped the fairy, zooming off down another aisle. "Good for making cavities and spare tires around your middle. Let's get some apples instead and some nice, juicy watermelon. While you're at it, throw some lettuce, beans, and carrots in the cart. Fruits and vegetables are the kind of high-test foods that are loaded with vitamins and minerals. You need vitamins and minerals to keep you healthy so you won't get colds and other virus infections."

"Oliver, you get some butter and vegetable oil. We all need a little fat in our diet to keep our bodies warm," said the fairy. "I'll find the potatoes and rice, and Olivia can get us some bread, cereal, and spaghetti. These foods are carbohydrates. Our bodies use carbohydrates to help digest fats and to provide us with quick energy."

When they were all finished shopping, the fairy said, "Make sure to eat the high-test foods we bought. I'll be back in a week to see how you're doing."

Then, in an instant, she was gone.

"Now, that's quick energy," marveled Olivia.

"She could have stuck around to help us put the groceries away," grumbled Oliver. "Whatever happened to fairies with magic wands?"

That night, at the dinner table, Oliver said, "I bet you can't do it."
"Do what?" asked Olivia.
"Give up potato chips and candy," he challenged.
"Look who's talking."
"I can do anything," boasted Oliver.
"We'll see," she replied.
So Olivia and Oliver spent the following week trying to prove who could be the best high-test-food eater. They drank plenty of natural fruit juices and had lots of raw vegetables and fruit for snacks.

Before they knew it, the week was over and the fairy bodmother appeared.

"I'm so proud of you," she said, beaming. "It took me much longer to give up all the low-test foods I used to love. You see, I used to be your typical, lazy fairy bodmother. I used my magic wand for everything. Now that I eat only high-test foods, I have so much energy, I like to do everything myself. I save the wand for special effects...like this:"

She waved the magic wand over each child's chest, saying:
"Abracadabra. Look out.
Here it comes.
My magic will let you
Look into your lungs."
"Wow!" squealed Oliver and Olivia as they gazed through each
other's chests.
"Some view!"
"Now take a deep breath," said the fairy.
"Oliver's lungs are filling up with air just like balloons,"
cried Olivia.
"They *are* like balloons," said the fairy bodmother.

"You breathe air in through your nose or your mouth and down through a tube in the back of your throat called your windpipe. Your windpipe carries the air into your lungs, where the other fuel your body needs is taken out. This fuel is called oxygen. Every cell in your body needs oxygen to live.

"There are millions of tiny tubes in your lungs called blood vessels. Blood vessels carry the oxygen mixed in with your blood to wherever it's needed. When you breathe out, your lungs get flatter as all the used-up air goes out the way it came in."

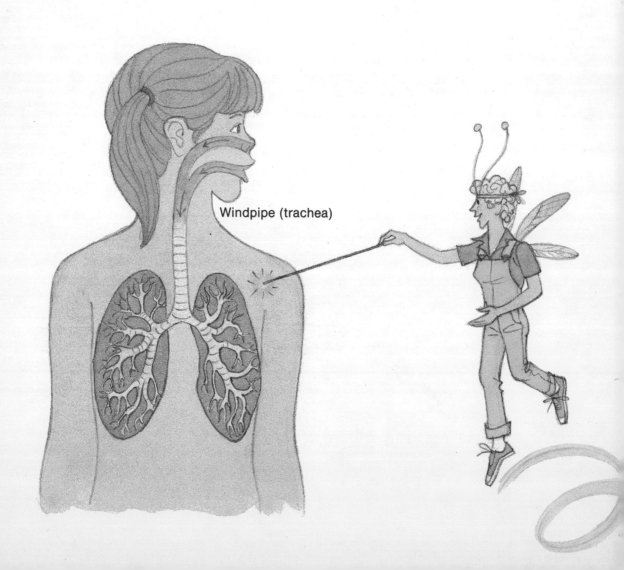

Windpipe (trachea)

"How does blood move?"
"What a good question, Oliver," said the fairy, smiling.
Then she waved her magic wand over their chests again, saying:
"Abracadabra.
Fill in the missing part.
In between your lungs,
I'll show you your heart."
"I can see Oliver's heart beating!" exclaimed Olivia.

"Each movement or beat of your heart sends blood through those large blood vessels that are attached to it. The large blood vessels are connected to smaller and smaller ones, the same way highways are connected to streets and roads. That's so the blood can get to every cell in your body."

"And the blood is filled with food and oxygen for fuel," added Oliver.

"Now you've got it!" said the fairy. "Every job your body does requires food and oxygen."

"Like a car needs gasoline to make it go!" said Olivia.

"Brilliant!" answered the fairy. "You kids are quick!"

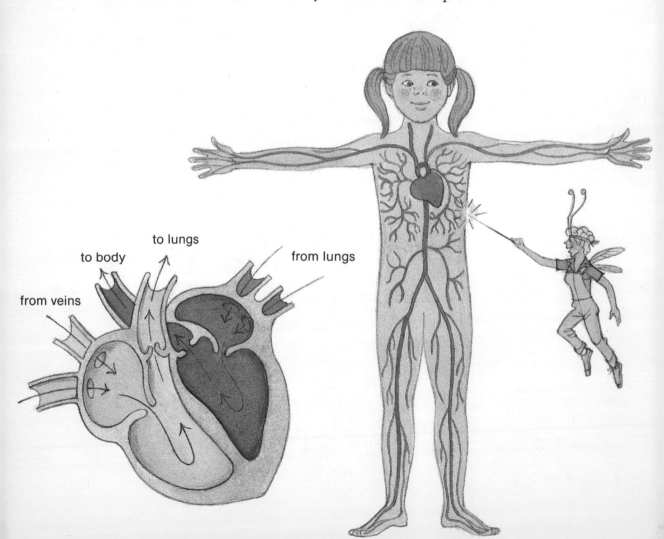

to lungs

to body

from lungs

from veins

"I know of a place where we can learn more about our bodies. Come with me to the amusement park."

"Like this?" objected Olivia, pointing at Oliver's chest. She could still see through it.

"Oops, I forgot," said the fairy, chuckling. And with a wave of her magic wand, they were ready to go.

"Let's walk there," suggested Olivia.

"What a high-test idea," said the fairy with a twinkle in her eye.

When they got to the amusement park, the fairy headed straight for the haunted house.

"Olivia, Oliver, meet Count Ribikov." She waved her wand over a pile of bones in the corner. Suddenly, they came to life.

"B-b-but he's a skeleton!" stuttered Oliver.

"And what's wrong with skeletons?" asked the count, looking annoyed. "Everybody has one. Your skeleton gives your body shape, and it protects organs like your heart and your brain. Bones are pretty amazing—if I do say so myself. They're very strong, yet light and easy to move around. Bones are light because they have tiny holes inside for blood vessels to fit through. Bones need to get fuel, too, especially calcium from milk to keep them strong."

"Very interesting, Count Ribikov," said the fairy as she waved her wand above him. "Have a nice rest now, dear," she added as he fell in a heap to the floor.

"Count Ribikov needs magic to make his bones move, but how do *we* lift our bones around?" asked Olivia.

"I know," said Oliver. "That's what muscles are for."

"Right," said the fairy. "Muscles are attached to bones."

"Wow! Look at that strongman over there!" exclaimed Olivia.

"Perfect," said the fairy. Then she waved the magic wand over him, saying, "Let's take a closer look—inside his skin."

"See how his muscles work?" she said. "When he lifts the dumbbell, the muscles in the inside of his upper arm tighten. At the same time, the muscles in the outside of his arm are relaxed. All muscles work in pairs that way. And the more you use them, the stronger they get.

"But muscles are not just for moving bones. Your heart is also a muscle, and you have breathing muscles in your chest, and muscles in your face to help you smile and frown. Because muscles are made of protein, we need to eat plenty of high-test foods to keep them healthy. What other type of fuel do your muscles need?" asked the fairy.

"Oxygen," replied Olivia.

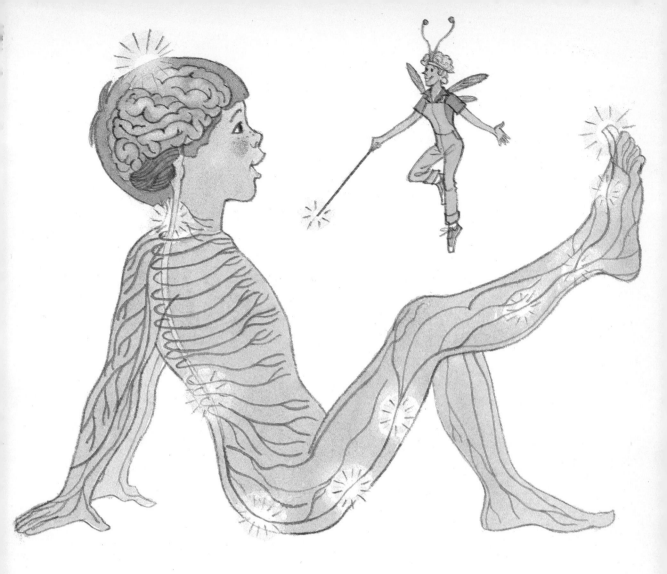

"How do muscles know what to do?" asked Oliver.

"Your brain tells them," answered the fairy. "Attached to your muscles are long nerves. They are like telephone wires that go up to your brain. When you want to wiggle your toe, your brain sends a message down one of those nerves that says, 'Tighten, relax, tighten, relax.' Your brain works like a super computer. Each part of it controls something that we do, think, or feel."

"One part figures out the messages that our eyes and ears send up. Our eyes take a picture of a round, bouncing thing, and our brain says, 'Ball.' Our ears hear a chirp, and our brain tells us, 'Bird.'

"Other parts of our brain help us to keep our balance, do our schoolwork, and feel pleasure and pain."

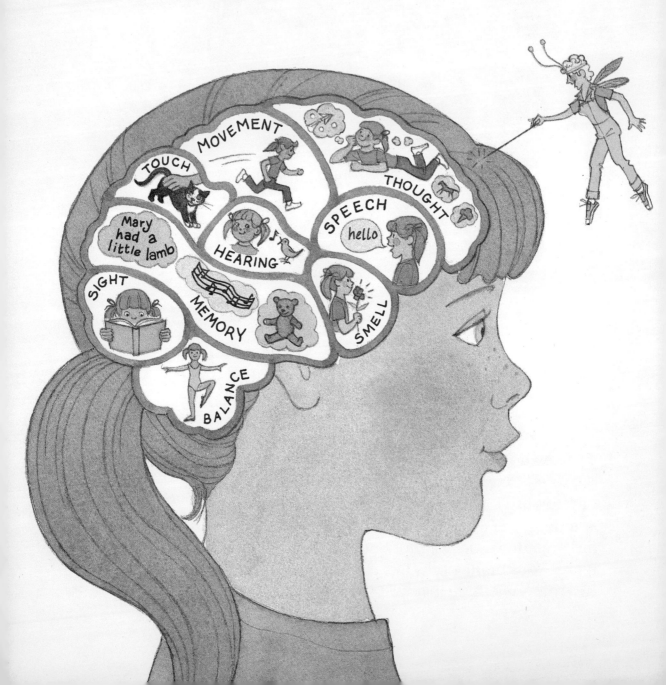

"Your brain never stops working. It tells your heart to beat and your lungs to breathe, even while you're sleeping. Sleep gives your muscles a chance to rest, and your body time to make new cells. That's why we wake up full of energy."

"My brain shows me pictures so I won't get too bored while I'm sleeping," said Oliver.

"You weren't bored last night," said Olivia. "I heard you yelling all the way down the hall. 'Give me one more chance! Please give me one more chance!'"

"Oh, that," said Oliver, blushing. "I dreamed I ate so much junk food that I turned into a jalopy!"

"I bet I know where that nightmare came from," said the fairy. "The monsters, goblins, and even 'jalopies' that sometimes appear in our nightmares are make-believe. They're really nothing more than our fears, worries, and wishes wearing disguises."

"But you don't have to worry about turning into a jalopy. You and Olivia are well on your way to becoming just like shiny, new sports cars," said the bodmother with a proud smile. Then suddenly, she did three double flips and buzzed to the window. "I've got to go now," she said. "There are still some jalopies out there that need plenty of body work."

In one blink, the tiny lady was gone.

"Who would believe it?" said Oliver.

"No one," answered Olivia, "but it doesn't matter. Now we know how to stay in shape—and that's what counts!"